LAURENCE FREEMAN OSB

Why are We Here?

Revised by Liam Kelly

CONVIVIUMPRESS

MEDITATIO

2012

Why are We Here?

© Laurence Freeman OSB

© Convivium Press 2012
All rights reserved
For the English Edition

http://www.conviviumpress.com
sales@conviviumpress.com
convivium@conviviumpress.com

7661 NW 68th St, Suite 108,
Miami, Florida 33166. USA.
Phone: +1 (305) 8890489
Fax: +1 (305) 8875463

Edited by Rafael Luciani
Revised by Liam Kelly
Designed by Eduardo Chumaceiro d'E
Series: *Meditatio*

ISBN: 978-1-934996-31-7

Printed in Colombia
Impreso en Colombia
D'VINNI, S.A.

Convivium Press
Miami, 2012

Why are We Here?

Contents

Why are We Here?

I'd like to talk about the monastic tradition of pure prayer, of Christian meditation. I'd like to begin with a prayer from St. Paul that contains the deepest theology of prayer. These words from St. Paul express that theology very beautifully in a prayer particularly addressed to the community.

> *I kneel in prayer to the Father, from whom every family in heaven and on earth takes its name, that out of the treasures of his glory he may grant you strength and power through his spirit in your inner being, so that through faith Christ may dwell in your hearts in love. With deep roots and firm foundations, may you be strong to grasp, with all God's people, what is the height and length and depth and breadth of the love of Christ, and to know it, though it is beyond knowledge. So may you come to fullness of being, the fullness of God himself (Eph. 3:14-19).*

2

❧

Why are we here? It's a very simple question. It's a question we have to come back to every day if we are to live a life of conversion. One of the Desert Fathers was asked, «What is a monk?» And the reply was, «A monk is someone who asks himself everyday what is a monk». We are all here because we have the work of God to do; we have to allow the work of God to be done in us. This is what St. Bernard called «the business of businesses» —the basic business, the basic work.

3

❧

The business of the Christian, no less than of the monk, is a very simple one. It is to open ourselves at the very centre of our being, to the source of our being. Not only to open it partially, but to open totally. Not only to open it some of the time, but to open it permanently. The purpose of the monk's life is to come to continuous prayer, to a state of

undistracted attention, to a state of unbroken open-
ness to the prayer of Christ in our hearts, to the
simple union of our prayer with the prayer of
Christ. This condition of unbroken prayer is the
purpose of our life, not only as monks but even
more deeply as Christians and as children of God.

4

This call to continuous prayer is as equally valid
today as it was in the 4th century in Egypt. No doubt
some of the means will be different, and some of
the styles in which we develop the means will be
new. But the essential means, which is prayer and
the ascesis of prayer and the simplicity of prayer,
must be the same; otherwise we are not part of the
tradition.

5

St. Benedict knew very well that this call to contemplative prayer, to continuous prayer, is not an

abstract call. The Rule of St Benedict is not a treatise on spirituality or theology of prayer. The Rule is about bringing people as quickly as possible and as painlessly as possible to this state of continuous prayer, to the breakthrough. St. Benedict, like the Buddha, realised that we come to this continuous prayer not through extremes, but through the middle way, and indeed through a way of love. That's why I think St. Benedict's Rule is so full of daily details, why he describes the daily difficulties of leaving our own wills behind. That he says is the first step and indeed the many-times repeated step of coming to this continuous prayer: to abandon our own wills, to leave self behind, to transcend our egos, to move beyond living as isolated beings —isolated in our wounds, isolated in our fears, isolated in our fantasies, isolated in our vanity, isolated in our anger, isolated in our jealousy. The purpose of the Rule, as of the whole Christian life, is to move beyond those prisons, emotional chains of isolation, into a state of communion, which is symbolised by the love that we have for one another and indeed realised by the love we have for one another.

6

Benedict sees the monastery of course as the work-shop for this most human of businesses which is prayer. Nothing must be preferred to the love of Christ; nothing must be preferred to prayer, because it is in prayer and the love of Christ within our hearts that we return to this first and basic step over and over again of leaving self behind: «Anyone who wishes to be a follower of mine must leave self behind». Both the Gospels and the Rule and the whole of our tradition make it very clear to us that if we see this call to continuous prayer as the essence of our vocation then we must never lose sight of that first step of leaving self behind.

7

We must always see ourselves as beginners, never as experts. Do not desire to be called holy until you really are holy. We must never even think of ourselves as experts, and perhaps not even think of anyone else as an expert. There is always the first step to go back to over and over again.

8

∽

That's why within the monastic life pre-eminently, but also in every life that is a life of prayer, there is this strong element of repetition, of a rhythm, of a cycle, something that goes over and over again —the wheel of prayer turning, turning, turning, not aimlessly, not mere repetition, but a rhythm of repetition that takes us forward just as the wheel turning over and over again moves the car or the carriage forward.

9

∽

Continuous prayer means continuous work and continuous encouragement. That I suppose is the psychological dynamic of a community, that it gives us the continuous encouragement we need to remain fresh in our vocation, to remain aware that we are taking the same step over and over again. Without that encouragement, I don't think it is humanly possible, except maybe for one in ten million, to make this journey seriously, fully or joyfully. So if we are committed, we've heard this call to continuous prayer taking us beyond our ego, we are open to encouragement, we are open to the wisdom of a tradition, and we are open to the love and support of others.

John Main at Gethsemani Abbey, 1976

In 1976, John Main who was my own teacher and novice master, friend, teacher, came to Gethsemani, I think in this room, and gave three conferences. In the first of them, he told the story of how he himself came to meditation. In the second conference, he spoke about the underlying Christian theology of meditation in the tradition of Cassian and the Desert Fathers in the Christian contemplative tradition. In the third conference, he had a discussion with the community here. After he returned to Ealing Abbey in England, he was sent a transcript of those three conferences and we read them together. He had already started a community, a small meditation centre at Ealing, and I suggested that this would be a very good little booklet to give to people. So we printed them and they have been known ever since as the *Gethsemani Talks*. They are still one of the best-selling books of John Main.

2

While Fr. John was here, he spent some time up at Merton's hermitage. While he was there, I think he came to a deep insight. He wrote in a letter to a friend of his from the hermitage that he had just celebrated the most loving mass of his life. It was during his time here that he came to the decision to accept an invitation from the Archbishop of Montreal to go there and establish a small centre of prayer. He phoned the Archbishop of Montreal from here and said that was what he had decided to do, and he would change his ticket and come back through Montreal to explore it further.

3

About eighteen months or maybe two years later, I went with him as a young monk with simple vows from Ealing to start a small centre of prayer in Montreal. Five years later, Fr. John died at the end of 1982. The community was still very small, rather fragile, but it had put down one very deep root. It was the root of prayer, and it was a root that began to spread. It spread to the extent that now what you might call a community of Christian meditators has come into being around the world. There are meditators meeting each week in small Christian meditation groups. They meet in parishes, in communities, in people's homes, in places of work, in schools, universities. They meet together for a little teaching, for a half-an-hour of silent meditation and for some sharing or mutual encouragement. That story, of which Gethsemani was a part, is the story of the expansion of a monastic tradition of prayer into the church at large.

x

ple, a consecrated nation, a royal priesthood. The letters of St. Paul describing the experience of the indwelling Christ are letters addressed to the very ordinary people of the early Christian churches.

We can see two very powerful movements in the Church today around the world. One of them is the option for the poor, the identification of the church with the needy, with the oppressed, with the great causes of peace and justice. But there is another complementary movement in the Church, which is the movement of contemplative awakening, contemplative deepening, contemplative renewal, the great search for deeper prayer. These two movements in the Church are clearly aspects of the same spirit, the same renewal, rebirth of Christ's Church. When we see men and women around the world committing themselves very deeply and seriously to a contemplative life, it gives us a new vision of the Church, the Church as a leaven, the church as salt, no longer the church as an imperial power but the church as the servant of the people of God.

6

About a year ago Bede Griffiths wrote an introduction to a collection of John Main's works, and he said that in his experience John Main was the best spiritual guide in the church today. He explained what he meant by saying that in the writings or thought of John Main, there were two very important insights for the modern Church: the insight that the renewal of the Church is a contemplative renewal at every level, and secondly the insight that the contemplative experience creates Christian community.

7

Many of you will be familiar with the way of meditation that John Main taught and that has created this community of Christian meditators. Let me just remind you of it briefly now. It's essentially a way of total simplicity. It's rooted of course in the teaching of Cassian in the Tenth Conference. Cassian talks about the great obstacle to pure prayer as the obstacle of our distractions and of our egoism. He recommends this wonderfully simple and ancient tradition of taking a single verse, or a single word even, and repeating this verse continually over and over again in the heart during the time of meditation. He says the monk, revolving this verse continuously in his heart, «comes with ready ease to that poverty of spirit which the Lord expresses as the first of the beatitudes» leaving behind all the riches of thought and imagination, moving beyond images of God into the pure presence of God in our hearts, moving beyond *my* prayer into the prayer of Christ. John Main had first learnt this way of meditation in the East. When he rediscovered it in his own Christian and monastic tradition, he recognised it and he went on to teach it, realising that this was a way of prayer of such simplicity that it was relevant to all ordinary people.

His teaching simplified it perhaps even more when he said: The way to meditate is to sit down, to sit still, to come to a stillness of body as well as a stillness of mind, to close your eyes lightly, and then silently, interiorly, in stillness, without moving your lips or your tongue, silently to repeat your word, your phrase. We call it a mantra. Cassian called it a formula in Latin. The mantra that John Main used to recommend was the Aramaic phrase, *maranatha*, the first and most ancient of Christian prayers. He advised you to say the word slowly, reciting it clearly in your heart and mind and listening to the word as you say it, so that the word leads you beyond the distractions of the mind into the silence of the heart —leads us beyond our ego-centric prayer, where there is so much of *I*, into the prayer of Christ. That is the practical and ordinary discipline of prayer that underlies the theory and the theology. But it is a simple and practical experience of prayer that also enriches our theology and our reading of scripture, and our life together, and our liturgy together.

We could just conclude now with some words from the Letter to the Ephesians which point us also towards the purpose and the meaning of our journey of prayer:

I pray that the God of our Lord Jesus Christ, the all glorious Father, may give you the spiritual powers of wisdom and vision, by which there comes the knowledge of him. I pray that your inward eyes may be illumined, so that you may know what is the hope to which he calls you, what the wealth and glory of the share he offers you among his people in their heritage, and how vast the resources of his power open to us who trust in him (Eph. 1:17-19).

Chapter 3

The Wakefulness of Prayer

1

From the Gospel of Matthew:

> *Keep awake then, for you do not know on what day*
> *your Lord is to come. Remember, if the householder had*
> *known at what time of night the burglar was coming,*
> *he would have kept awake and not have let his house be*
> *broken into. Hold yourselves ready therefore because the*
> *Son of Man will come at the time you least expect him*
> *(Matt. 24:42-44).*

I'd like to reflect with you on the wakefulness of prayer, of meditation, and on the practical advice that the tradition gives us to come to that progressive awakening.

2

Part of the mystery of the church in our own time is the contemplative awakening that is taking place throughout the church. This contemplative awakening is making us all realise that this Holy Spirit that is our direct path into the Kingdom is placed within the heart and soul of each of us. Each of us is a temple of that Holy Spirit. Meditation is the lost chord of modern Christianity. The Western church in particular lost this contemplative dimension. From about the seventeenth century, prayer in the Western church was limited really to mental prayer. There came an increasing suspicion of contemplative prayer. The Western church, with the Western tendency to action rather than contemplation, became the great missionary church. This loss of the contemplative dimension was less acute in the Eastern church. In the Western church we can see, by contrast with the Eastern church, a spirituality that was centred very largely around the passion of Christ, whereas in the Eastern church the great focal point for spirituality scripturally would be the Transfiguration or the Resurrection. What we're talking about of course is achieving a balance, the great *harmonia*, the great harmony that is the Christian way. It is this recovery and awakening of the contemplative dimension in Christianity today that I think is restoring us to balance, to integrity.

3

It's the monastic tradition largely in the West that has picked up this lost chord —Merton being one of the great awakeners of this contemplative dimension, John Main giving a specific teaching on how to enter that contemplative dimension. So it is important to remember that meditation in the Christian tradition is not a new technique. Our own monastic tradition authenticates the integrity of the Christian nature of meditation. It's not a new technique or an Eastern import. We only have to look at the teaching of Cassian to see this.

4

In the Ninth Conference, Cassian begins his great teaching on prayer to Abbot Isaac and he describes a spectrum of prayer. He talks about prayer as taking different forms —petition, intercession, thanksgiving and so on, following St. Paul's list of types of prayer. But he also sees that this spectrum of prayer is progressive— it's moving in a certain direction. These different forms of prayer have a direction. They are pointing always to what he comes to call «pure prayer», prayer that is beyond images of God.

5

~

St. Gregory of Nyssa said every concept of God is an idol. Even St. Thomas Aquinas said God is nothing that can be thought. *The Cloud of Unknowing* says: «By thought we cannot know him, but only by love». There's nothing strange in the Christian tradition that prayer moves us ultimately beyond thought, because God, who is the goal and the aim of prayer, is himself beyond thought, images, ideas.

6

~

When we come to think of meditation, it is helpful to have some general idea of the whole spectrum of prayer. Instead of a spectrum, we could think of prayer as a great wheel. The different spokes in the wheel are the different forms of prayer. As many forms as you like to think of, as many ways of prayer as you can imagine, from the rosary to the Eucharist to the liturgy of the hours, to scriptural prayer, to petitionary prayer, to intercessory prayer. Every type of prayer you like to think of could be included among those spokes. The outer rim of the wheel is rather like our life, the edge that makes contact with the earth, the wheel that turns and takes us forward. But all these spokes of the wheel are connected and come together at the centre of the wheel, the hub of the wheel. And there, is stillness. At the hub of the wheel, there is stillness. The outer rim moves, but the centre of the hub is still. And that central hub of the wheel of prayer is simply the prayer of Christ himself.

7

The basic theology of all Christian prayer is that our journey of prayer is beyond our own prayer, beyond our egocentric prayer, into the prayer of Christ himself: «I live no longer but Christ lives in me». «We do not know how to pray, but the Spirit prays within us».

8

36

We could say that meditation forms the interface between all the different spokes of the wheel and the hub of the wheel, the prayer of Christ. It is in meditation or pure prayer, the prayer that takes us beyond thought and ultimately beyond the ego, that it is, as it were, the final step, the step that is the result of grace, not effort, but the final step from ourselves into Christ. Cassian clearly shows that this pure prayer is related to all the other forms of prayer. You don't have to give up any other form of prayer that you find useful if you decide to make meditation an integral part of your spiritual life.

The Distracted Mind

1

In the Tenth Conference Cassian gets down to earth. He starts talking in practical terms about how we deal with the distracted mind. Somebody once compared the mind to a tree full of monkeys, jumping from branch to branch shouting and chattering to each other. We all know that a little below the surface of our conscious minds we have immense distraction. He talks about the problem of distraction.

2

For the Desert Fathers, distractedness is almost the same as original sin. They were horrified that they'd gone out into the desert, they'd given up everything, they practised great austerity and asceticism, and still they could not make it. One realises just how horrified they were by the discovery of their own distractedness. So the great question for Cassian in the Tenth Conference is: How do we get beyond this wandering mind, this distracted and fickle mind; how do we move beyond the images and the thoughts that are constantly passing through that surface level of consciousness?

3

∽

Cassian at that point teaches the tradition of the mantra in Christianity. He calls it a «formula», a short verse. He says this tried and tested tradition (he insists upon the authority of this tradition as going back to apostolic times) is a tried and tested practice to lead the mind from its distractedness to stillness. «Take a single verse». He recommends: Oh God come to my assistance. «Repeat it continually», he says «over and over again, revolving it in the heart. And by the constant repetition of the single verse you will come with ready ease to that first of the beatitudes, to poverty of spirit».

It's certainly true that we can find this very simple method taking us beyond distraction, taking us to depth of consciousness, in other religions. But, here, at the heart of Christian spiritual tradition, we find it expressed in scriptural terms, in terms of Christian theology. The repetition of the single verse leads us to poverty of spirit, the renunciation of all thoughts and imagination, ultimately all sense of ego, because it leads us from that poverty of spirit into the Kingdom of heaven, the prayer of Christ which is within us. This poverty is the key theological idea or scriptural idea that Cassian plays with when he describes meditation, pure prayer.

5

Meditation is a path. It's a discipline. It isn't a technique. A technique is something that we practise with the ego in order to achieve a desired result, and to be in control of the whole process. With a disci-

pline, we are transcending the ego. We are not prac-
tising a discipline in order to get a desired result, but
in order to lose ourselves, to move from the ego to
the true self. No one can find his true self, Jesus
tells us, unless we lose our false self.

6

∾

42 Meditation, when practised as a discipline, is not a
matter of mastering a theory. Nor is it a matter of
mastering a technique. There's very little technique,
when you think about it, to this way of prayer
—the repetition in the heart of a single verse.
There's a very simple practical usefulness about
learning to say the mantra in rhythm with your
breathing, as with the Jesus prayer for example. The
Jesus prayer is clearly the mantra of the Orthodox
Church. If you take a single word, it's useful probably to say the mantra as you breathe in, on the in
breath, and then breathe out in silence. Let the
mantra rest on the breath as it comes in and breathe
out in silence. But basically, you find your own way
of saying it. And basically in this tradition, you

would pay attention not to the breath but to the mantra to the word, listening to the sound of the word, rather than either watching what is happening or watching your breath.

Chapter 5

The Power of the Mantra

1

Cassian talks about the great change in us that this way of prayer begins to unfold. It becomes a part of a whole way of life, not just a way of prayer, but a way of life of re-centring our life away from the ego and on the spirit or the true self.

2

Cx

The essential work of the mantra is to bring the mind to stillness, to stop us thinking about ourselves. That's the simple work of all ascetical practice —to take us beyond self-consciousness, self-centredness, self-fixation. But it does so with gentleness; there is no force or violence. If we use force or violence, then we are using a technique. A technique is in the control of the ego. And how can the ego transcend the ego? Therefore the way of prayer we follow to transcend the ego must be itself an egoless way, a gentle way, a way in which we let go of control while at the same time committing ourselves to a discipline. To follow this on a daily basis becomes the following of a spiritual path. And I think it soon begins to teach us some of the characteristics of the spirit in a new and fresh kind of way.

3

The spiritual is something that cannot be measured. We can measure most things that we do. We can measure how much we produce in a factory; we can measure our progress in learning a language; we can measure the results of a slimming diet; we can measure even our religious practice to some extent —we talk about how observant somebody is, how many times they go to church. But the spiritual is something that by its nature cannot be measured. Spirit is like the wind, Jesus tells us. It comes from where we do not know, and it goes we do not know where. We see its effect. We see the wind blowing in the trees but we cannot measure where it has come from or where it is going. In this way, too, we cannot measure our progress in this way of prayer.

We will see the fruits of it above all in our daily life. Living in community one sees the fruits of it most evidently I think in our relationships with each other. One of the most common fruits of this kind of prayer, I think, is a person's awareness, usually to their great surprise, that they are becoming more tolerant, more patient, even more compassionate, less judgemental, less irritated, less isolated. Simply because in this work of the mantra, we are unhooking ourselves from the ego at its root. This is why *The Cloud of Unknowing,* the little treatise on Christian meditation, on the mantra, in the same tradition as Cassian, calls this prayer the time of the work, and it also says that in this work we go to the very root of sin. *The Cloud* even goes so far as to say that it is more effective than all other penances because it goes to the very root of sin, our ego.

5

Cassian talks about the mantra as a fixed mark upon which the mind can focus to bring it to stillness. *The Cloud of Unknowing* talks of the mantra as like a dart with which we beat upon the cloud of unknowing. In the Indian tradition the mantra is somewhere described as like the bow that fires the arrow of the self into the heart of God. John Main described the mantra as like a radar bleep that brings a plane in to land through thick fog. Even when you don't know where you are going, if you can stay tuned on that radar signal you know that it will bring you in to land.

6

Why should the mantra be said continuously during the time of meditation? Cassian and *The Cloud* are very clear about this continuous recitation of the mantra. Cassian says: say it whatever happens, keep returning to it. In the Tenth Conference he goes through a great list of possible experiences, moods and feelings that we go through as we pray —the seasons of the soul, the moods, the temperaments that we have. And at the end of each description he says: Say this verse, keep saying the mantra. «Say it in prosperity and in adversity», he says. The reason is, I think, if we can understand the purpose of the mantra, it's not simply to bring us to quiet, not simply to make us feel a sense of euphoria or well-being, but to go to the very root of our ego and ultimately to lead us, in God's own time and by grace, beyond the narrow limited world of the ego, beyond the orbit of the ego around which we are usually revolving.

7

∽

There comes perhaps a time, when we stop saying the mantra, when we are led into pure silence, pure simplicity. But it is very important for us I think to be cautious about how we understand that. The purpose of the mantra is not just to lead us to quiet but to lead us beyond the ego, beyond all sense of

«I». That's why a very simple way of describing this would be to say: «Say your word until you can no longer say it. We do not choose when to stop saying it. And as soon as you realise that you have stopped saying it, then simply start saying it again». When we are meditating and we are led into a state of quiet, there may be no distractions or very few distractions and we feel very peaceful, and then we say to ourselves, «I am silent. I don't need to say the mantra anymore». The problem of course is that if we say we are silent, we are breaking the silence. The thought «I am silent» is a sign that we have not fully become simple, totally simple; we are still self reflective. And there is the radical simplicity of Cassian's teaching, why he insists to say the mantra in times of adversity and in times of prosperity. The purity of prayer relies or depends upon this radical simplicity, the radical renunciation of our false identification with our ego.

〜

Cassian warns against two great dangers in prayer: the *sopor lethalis,* the lethal sleep, and the *pax perniciosa,* the pernicious peace —that state of kind of drowsy slightly piously stoned feeling, euphoria perhaps but a lack of wakefulness. The mantra leads us through the dangers of falling asleep. Cassian talks about this formula or the mantra as concentrating everything that we are, bringing it to unity, to focus. He said this little word, this verse, embraces everything that can be thought or felt. There's no sense here in which we are rejecting any part of ourselves or suppressing any part of ourselves. There's here the sense of the integration and the unification of our being.

Purity of Heart

1

Let's begin with these words of Jesus from the Gospel of Matthew:

> *The disciples came to Jesus and asked, «Who is the greatest in the kingdom of heaven?» He called a child set him in front of them and said, «I tell you this: unless you turn round and become like children you'll never enter the Kingdom of heaven. Let a man humble himself till he is like this child and he will be the greatest in the Kingdom of heaven».*

2

The goal of the monastic life according to the early fathers is uninterrupted prayer. Any discipline of prayer such as the discipline of meditation, the discipline of the mantra, is a way to that goal. Clearly there is more than one way to that goal.

3

※

In this discipline of pure prayer, the mantra, the formula of Cassian, unhooks us from the compulsive state of distractedness that the early fathers saw as the essential sinfulness of the human condition. It overcomes this compulsive distractedness because it calms the mind, brings it to stillness: «Be still and know that I am God». It focuses the mind, focuses our whole self bringing us to that simplicity, singleness of heart which is the real meaning of purity of heart.

4

※

So the mantra, the formula, is not a magic pill, it's not a technique; it's a discipline that has to be integrated within a whole spiritual awareness and system. Clearly, in Cassian's Tenth Conference, this method of prayer grows out for example of the monastic practice of *lectio* in which we read scripture not merely with the rational and analytical mind but with more of an intuitive and listening heart. In l*ectio*, it's very commonly practiced of course to take short sections of the passage that we are reading and rather than trying to get through twenty pages every *lectio* period we'll be quite happy perhaps to stay with one phrase or a couple of verses and chew them over. The early fathers said ruminate. So what could be more natural than to move on, as Cassian recommends, to an even simpler stage of prayer where we select a single verse or a single word from scripture and remain continuously with that at a certain level and time of prayer.

5

For Cassian, the formula or the mantra that grows out of our immersion in scripture becomes rooted in our heart by constant use. By the constant repetition and revolution of this verse in the heart, he says, it roots itself deep in our consciousness. He says you will go to sleep at night repeating this verse; you will wake in the morning repeating it. This is the prayer of the heart that never sleeps. I sleep but my heart is awake. This prayer of the heart is the essence of pure prayer. It links us to the essential theology of all Christian prayer that it is the goal of the Christian to become one, body mind and spirit, with the prayer of Christ which is in the human heart.

The heart once awakened never sleeps; the door once opened never closes; the day of Christ once it has dawned has no end. This is the continuous prayer that is the goal of the monk and indeed the goal of the Christian, according to St. Paul —to pray without ceasing. Which means not that we go around saying prayers all the time. That would create an alternative reality. We would end up simply in a state of isolation psychologically and spiritually if we thought that continuous prayer meant that *we* are saying prayers all day. Continuous prayer surely means the continuous prayer, the eternal prayer, timeless prayer of Jesus Christ: his glorified humanity awakened eternally to the father and worshipping the father in the spirit. Our continuous prayer is our entry, our union, our integration with his prayer, making the journey with him, he who went beyond himself to the Father finding himself in the Father as the Son but then returning to us in the Spirit, picking us up with him as it were on his return.

7

This is the theology that underlies the very simple practice of pure prayer that Cassian recommends. It's a way of simplicity. The word simple, in Latin *simplex,* was a tailoring term used by tailors and it referred to a piece of cloth that was unfolded. That is a simple thing —when you just unfold it. When it is folded, it becomes *duplex* or *complex.* That is the essence of pure prayer that it simplifies our mind, it opens our mind. When the mind is reflected upon itself, when we are thinking about ourselves, then we are complex, unchildlike.

The great quality of a child is simplicity. A child is not thinking about itself. What is so wonderful about a child is its unselfconsciousness. What is so refreshing about a child is its unselfconsciousness. What's so refreshing about holy people is their unselfconsciousness. I met Mother Teresa recently. We had a couple of meetings with her, which was a great privilege and most interesting, because she has one thought in her mind and that is her work and nothing gets in the way of it. Yet she has this incredible power of attention, of being present. Whoever she is with, she gives total attention to, and she brings that attention either to the poor and the sick or to the sisters or to the visitors. It's that quality of child-likeness that shines forth in her particular type of sanctity. There are different types of holiness, but a common characteristic of holiness seems to be that quality of childlike attention and simplicity, the unselfconsciousness. Perhaps that is the meaning of the traditional devotion to the child Jesus. It isn't that Jesus is this harmless little infant, but the child Jesus represents to us, especially within the Christmas liturgy, the essential childlikeness of the human condition. Yet this way of simplicity is not easy.

9

The mantra is not a magic pill. It's more like a pure stream of water that cleanses whatever it passes through, and it wears down the hardest stone. We soon meet resistance when we begin this journey to the heart, this way of simplicity. We meet many hindrances. We prayed this morning for perseverance for those on this contemplative journey. Perseverance seems to be the great call of the New Testament: stay firm, be firm, stay rooted; persevere, do not turn back. Walter Hilton in the 14th century wrote a book called *The Scale of Perfection* and in it he describes rather graphically the kind of experience that we all have I suppose when we first start this more interior way of prayer, when we move from the mind to the heart. He said it's like a man coming home after a hard day's work in the fields.

When he gets to his house he finds a smoking fire and a nagging wife and he runs out of the house as quickly as he can. *The Cloud* talks about the need to persevere at this work. Jesus, of course, gives us many words encouraging us to persevere, not to turn back, not to take our hand off the plough. A saint is a sinner who never gives up.

A New Attitude to Sin and God

1

This work of simplicity has a very profound and rather unexpected result fairly quickly. It soon begins to change our attitude to sin.

2

We begin to experience the interior resistance to becoming a child, to becoming simple, the clash as it were between our essential simplicity and our familiar complexities. We begin to see that sin is not so much a transgression that has to be punished, but it's a hindrance that has to be transcended. Not so much something that has to be punished, a breaking of the rule that has to be punished, but a block within ourselves that has to be cleared. I think we begin to read the words of scripture, the word *sin* in scripture for example, with a new sense, a new meaning. Cassian says, you remember, in the Tenth Conference, that the monk who has begun to pray in this way begins to read scripture with new eyes,

as if he is the author of the words. He begins to an-
ticipate the sense; he begins to resonate on the same
frequency as the word of God in scripture. We begin
to understand, in other words, from experience.
And our experience of sin becomes very real, but I
think more focused.

3

At this stage we are probably likely to maybe blame
the devil for fewer things and blame our ego for
more. We begin to see that the hindrances to our
childlikeness, to our simplicity, are in fact our teach-
ers in an unexpected form. They have something
very real and important to teach us about ourselves. Rather than things that have to be repressed,
crushed or ignored and denied, these hindrances
within ourselves, our egotistical hindrances, become things that reveal something very true about
us. Remember St. Anthony of the Desert, at the end
of his temptations and struggles with the devil,
came to the surprising conclusion that even the
devil had something good in him.

4

The hindrances that we experience could be described as the seven deadly sins. Cassian was the first in the Christian tradition to formulate that list, and we can add our own refinements to it: anger; irritability; vindictiveness; desire; self-indulgence —the way we use pleasure to escape reality; laziness—physical, mental, spiritual; envy of all kinds —material, psychological, emotional; pride, even the kind of pride that lurks behind the humble exterior, the pride in our own humility or the appearance of our own humility; greed where we want to acquire probably not material things. That's perhaps the meaning of confession, the sacrament of reconciliation: to make us aware of these hindrances that each of us has in a unique formula, a unique recipe according to our own temperament, hindrances that we are very quick to recognize and label in others but that we ourselves perhaps are usually ignorant about or vague about. And perhaps ignorance is one of the greatest hindrances of all, our lack of self-awareness.

This new understanding of sin as something that blocks us or complicates us and hinders us from this journey to simplicity, as something that simply interrupts the state of continuous prayer or interrupts our entry into the prayer of Christ, begins also I think to change our understanding of God. If our understanding of sin begins to change, if we see that sin is something that blocks us rather than being the breaking of a rule, sin as something that blocks us from the state of a child, our true state, then we begin to see that God does not punish us. I think most of us have received early in our lives an image of God as one who punishes. Intellectually, theologically we may have changed that image, but emotionally, psychologically probably that image still has some force in us and creates a certain fear, an unhealthy fear. But I think this pure prayer, bringing us to self-knowledge as it does, also brings us to the knowledge of God, and therefore to the awareness that God does not punish us for our sin. St. Augustine said every disordered soul is its own punishment. Sin contains its own punishment; God doesn't have to add fuel to the fire of hell.

Three Simple Rules

1

There are three very simple rules that one might describe as guiding us on this way of meditation which is always a way of beginning.

2

The first of them is to have no demands or expectations about what's going to happen, and indeed if anything does happen ignore it. I think in that there's a simple description of poverty of spirit —having no demands or expectations and letting go of anything that might happen.

3

Secondly, it's not to compare our experience with anybody else's, whether it is St. John of the Cross or Thomas Merton or John Main or the person sitting next to you. We don't have to compare our experience with anybody. We can learn from other people but it isn't valuable to compare. Each of us has a unique identity. Each of us is called into a unique place in the Kingdom of God.

4

Finally, it's to live our meditation, in other words, not to separate the times of meditation, morning and evening perhaps, not to separate them from our life but to see that they are interwoven, and that the fruits of the meditation are to be found in our daily living. So it isn't at the time of meditation that we should be looking for results but at our life itself. And quite probably it will be by the reflection of others that we really see what change is taking place.

Why are We Here?

This book was printed on *thin opaque smooth white Bible paper*, using the *Minion* and *Type Embellishments One* font families.

This edition was printed in D'VINNI, S.A., in Bogotá, Colombia, during the last weeks of the fourth month of year two thousand twelve.

Ad publicam lucem datus mensis aprilis,
festivitatem Divina Misericordia